The Life and Work of...

Edgar Degas

Jayne Woodhouse

www.heinemann.co.uk/library
Visit our website to find out more information about Heinemann Library books.

To order:
 Phone 44 (0) 1865 888066
 Send a fax to 44 (0) 1865 314091
Visit the Heinemann Bookshop at www.heinemann.co.uk/library to browse our catalogue and order online.

First published in Great Britain by Heinemann Library, Halley Court, Jordan Hill, Oxford OX2 8EJ, a division of Reed Educational and Professional Publishing Ltd. Heinemann is a registered trademark of Reed Educational & Professional Publishing Ltd.

OXFORD MELBOURNE AUCKLAND JOHANNESBURG BLANTYRE
GABORONE IBADAN PORTSMOUTH (NH) USA CHICAGO

Designed by Celia Floyd
Illustrations by Karin Littlewood
Originated by Ambassador Litho Ltd
Printed and bound in Hong Kong/China

ISBN 0 431 09210 9

06 05 04 03 02
10 9 8 7 6 5 4 3 2 1

British Library Cataloguing in Publication Data

Woodhouse, Jayne
    The life and work of Edgar Degas
    1. Degas, Edgar, 1834–1917
    2. Painters – France – Biography – Juvenile literature
    3. Painting – France – Juvenile literature
    I. Title
    II. Edgar Degas
    759.4

J137,520
£10.15

Acknowledgements
The Publisher would like to thank the following for permission to reproduce photographs: Bibliothéque Nationale: pp4, 18, 22, 24, 28; Bridgeman Art Library: Barber Institute of Fine Arts, University of Birmingham p19, Fitzwilliam Museum, University of Cambridge p29, Musée des Beaux-Arts, Pau, France p17, Musée d'Orsay, Paris p11, Musée d'Orsay, Paris/Giraudon p21, Municipal Museum of Art, Kitakyushu, Japan/Giraudon p13, National Gallery, London p15, Peter Willi/Louvre, Paris p9, Peter Willi/Musée d'Orsay, Paris p7; Christies Images: pp25, 27; corbis: p16; National Gallery of Art, Washington: p23; RMN – H Lewandowski: p26; Roger Viollet/Musée d'Orsay, Paris: p5.

Cover photograph (Blue Dancers, Edgar Degas) reproduced with permission of The Art Archive/Musée d'Orsay, Paris/Dagli Orti.

Every effort has been made to contact copyright holders of any material reproduced in this book. Any omissions will be rectified in subsequent printings if notice is given to the Publisher.

Any words appearing in the text in bold, **like this**, are explained in the Glossary.

Contents

Who was Edgar Degas?

Edgar Degas was a French artist. He worked with a group of artists called the **Impressionists**. He used paintings, drawings, **sculpture** and photography to show his ideas.

Edgar lived all his life in **Paris**. His pictures show the people and places he saw around him. His most famous paintings are of ballet dancers. He finished this one when he was 38.

Dance Class at the Opéra, 1872

Early years

Edgar was born in **Paris**, on 19 July 1834. He came from a rich family. He was the eldest of five children. When Edgar was a boy, his father Auguste often took him to visit art **galleries**.

Edgar's father did all he could to help Edgar become an artist. Some years later, Edgar painted Auguste as an old man. He loved listening to music.

Lorenzo Pagans and Auguste de Gas, about 1871–72

Learning to be an artist

When he was 19, Edgar began studying law but he soon gave it up to be an artist. He loved the work of painters known as the **Old Masters**, and spent hours copying their paintings.

Some of Edgar's early pictures were **self-portraits**. Here he is aged about 20. He shows himself as a well-dressed, rather shy-looking, young man.

Portrait of the Artist, 1855

Travels in Italy

During his twenties, Edgar travelled in Italy to learn more about art. He filled lots of sketchbooks with copies of the great paintings he saw there.

Bellelli Family, 1858–67

In Italy, Edgar stayed with his aunt. He did many drawings of his relatives, which he later made into this painting. Edgar found many clever ways to show they were not a happy family.

An important meeting

One day, in 1862, Edgar was copying a painting in the **Louvre** in **Paris**. There he met an artist called Edouard Manet. They shared many ideas about art and became good friends.

However, Edgar and Edouard sometimes fell out. Edgar painted this picture of Edouard and his wife as a gift. He was very angry when Edouard cut out the part he didn't like!

Monsieur and Madame Manet, about 1868

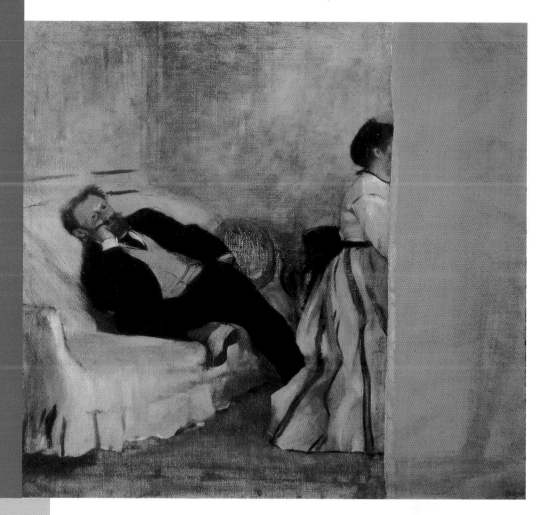

Sharing ideas

Edouard introduced Edgar to other artists who we now call the **Impressionists**. The artists often met in a café to discuss art. They held **exhibitions** together many times.

However, Edgar's ways of working were very different from the Impressionists. They painted outside, from real life. Edgar worked in his **studio**, from his **sketches** and memory. This is how he made this beach scene.

Young Girl being Combed by her Maid, 1876–77

Travels in America

When Edgar was 38, he visited New Orleans, in America. Other members of his family lived there. He stayed at his uncle's house.

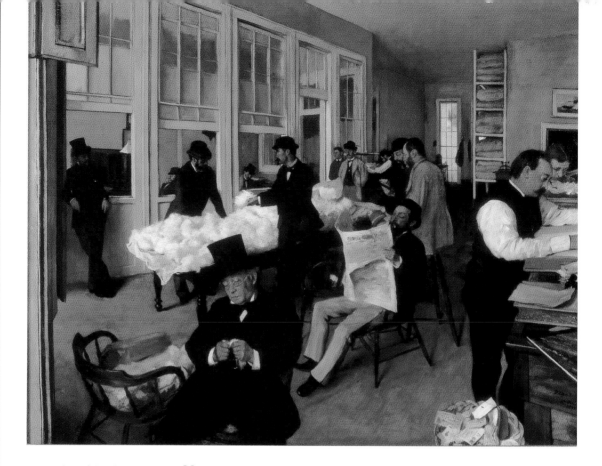

Portraits in an Office, New Orleans, 1873

Edgar painted the cotton office where his relatives worked. His grandfather is seated at the front, and his brother is reading a newspaper. This was the first of Edgar's pictures to be bought by an art **gallery**.

17

Friendships

Edgar never married, but he had close friends he would often visit. These were happy times, as this photograph shows. Edgar is the figure on the right.

Some of his friends lived near a **racecourse**. Edgar made many pictures of horses and jockeys. This one, painted from behind the wooden post, shows how he liked to paint from unusual viewpoints.

Jockeys Before the Race, about 1878–79

19

Edgar the observer

Edgar wanted to show real life as he saw it happening. He always carried a notebook with him. He used to write about and draw the things he saw.

Edgar was interested in the lives of ordinary people, especially women. In his forties and fifties, he painted workers in a **laundry**. He took great care to make the pictures as accurate as possible.

Laundresses, about 1884–86

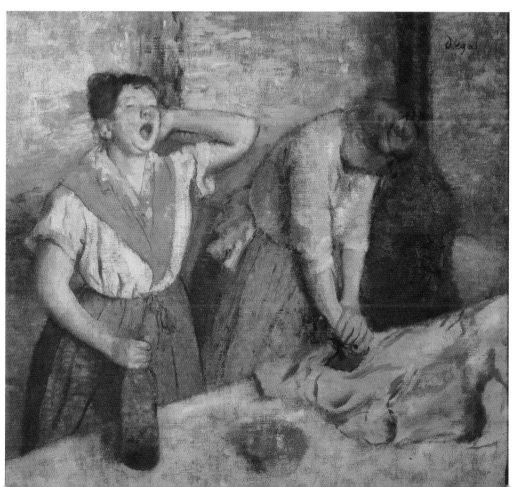

Photographs

During Edgar's lifetime, photography was invented. Edgar was always looking for new ideas. When he was about 60, he bought a camera and began to take photographs. He took this one in his **studio**.

Sometimes Edgar traced over his photographs to get the movements of the dancers right. He worked on his pictures for a long time, but they often look like **snapshots**.

Four Dancers, about 1899

Sculptures

Edgar often made models in wax and clay to try out ideas for his pictures. From about 1890 his eyesight began to fail and painting was difficult. **Sculpture** became even more important to him.

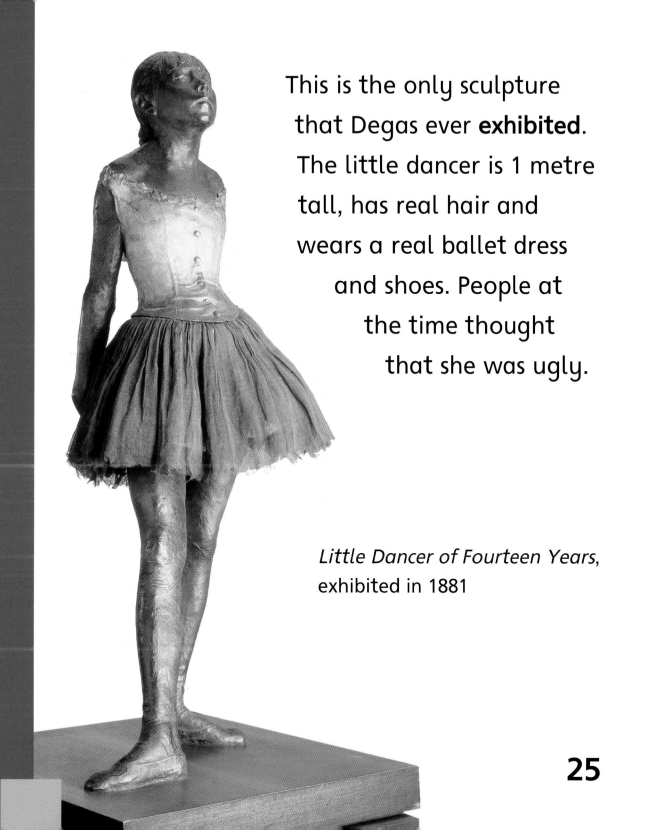

This is the only sculpture that Degas ever **exhibited**. The little dancer is 1 metre tall, has real hair and wears a real ballet dress and shoes. People at the time thought that she was ugly.

Little Dancer of Fourteen Years, exhibited in 1881

Pastels

Edgar liked to work with many different materials. He was one of the few artists of his time to use sticks of colour called pastels. This box of pastels was found in his **studio**.

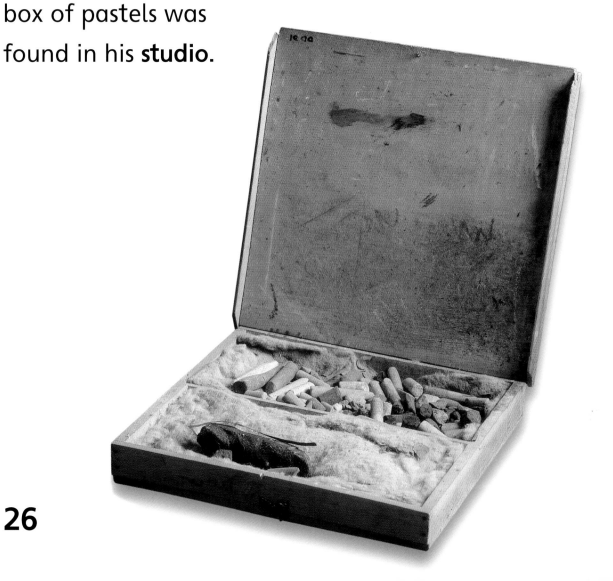

This picture of Russian dancers was done in pastels. As Edgar's sight grew worse, the colours of his pictures became stronger and brighter.

Russian Dancers, 1899

Edgar's last years

For the last five years of his life Edgar was nearly blind. He stopped working completely. He spent hours each day walking the streets of **Paris**, a sad and lonely man.

Edgar died in 1917, aged 83. After his death, about 150 wax figures were found in his **studio**. Many were later made into **bronze** and put on display. Today Edgar's work can be seen in **galleries** all around the world.

Ballet Dancer, Bronze

29

Timeline

1834	Edgar Degas is born in **Paris**, France on 19 July.
1847	Edgar's mother dies.
1853	He studies law for a short time and begins to copy paintings in the **Louvre**.
1855	He studies art at the School of Fine Arts in Paris.
1856–60	Edgar travels in Italy.
1862	He meets Edouard Manet.
1865	Edgar buys a **studio** in Montmartre, in Paris.
1870	France at war with Prussia, which was part of Germany.
1871–72	Edgar travels to London and New Orleans.
1874	His father dies.
	The first **Impressionist exhibition** takes place.
1880s	Edgar becomes friends with the American painter Mary Cassatt.
	From this time, he becomes more and more famous. His works are exhibited all over the world.
1890	Edgar moves to a new studio.
	From now on, his sight becomes worse. He works more in **sculpture** and in pastels.
1895	He begins to experiment with photography.
1912	Edgar moves from his studio.
	He is now almost blind and stops working.
1914	The start of World War I.
1917	Edgar dies at his home on 27 September, aged 83.

Glossary

bronze   a type of metal

exhibition   works of art on display for people to see

gallery   room or building where works of art are shown

Impressionists   group of artists who showed the effect of light and movement in their pictures

laundry   place where clothes are washed and ironed

Louvre   museum and art gallery in Paris

Old Masters   famous artists from Europe who lived a long time ago

Paris   capital city of France

racecourse   place where people go to see horses racing

sculpture   piece of art made from stone, wood, clay or metal

self-portrait   picture an artist makes of himself or herself

sketch   unfinished or rough drawing or painting

snapshot   natural looking photograph taken quickly

studio   special room or building where an artist works

More books to read

An Introduction to Degas, Peter Harrison, Hodder Wayland

Degas: The Invisible Eye, Great Artists, David Spence, Ticktock

Websites

www.ibiblio.org/wm/paint/auth/ degas/ballet – shows many of Degas' paintings of ballet dancers.

More paintings to see

Ballet Dancers, Edgar Degas, National Gallery, London

In a Café, Edgar Degas, Musée d'Orsay, Paris

Woman Ironing, Edgar Degas, Walker Art Gallery, Liverpool

Index

Titles in the *Life and Work of* series include:

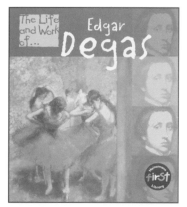

Hardback   0 431 09210 9

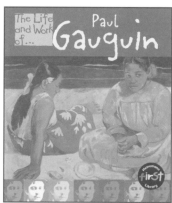

Hardback   0 431 09216 8

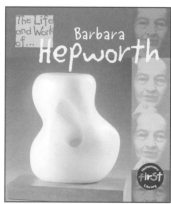

Hardback   0 431 09212 5

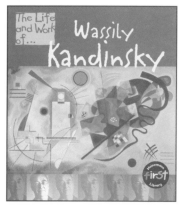

Hardback   0 431 09217 6

Hardback   0 431 09218 4

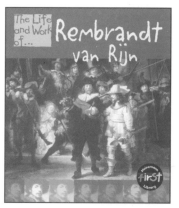

Hardback   0 431 09211 7

Hardback   0 431 09219 2

Find out about the other titles in this series on our website www.heinemann.co.uk/library